To Michael

KINGFISHER BOOKS
Grisewood & Dempsey Inc.
95 Madison Avenue
New York, New York 10016

First American Edition 1992

2 4 6 8 10 9 7 5 3 1

Library of Congress Cataloging-in-Publication Data
applied for.

ISBN 1–85697–823–0

Edited by Camilla Hallinan
Designed by The Pinpoint Design Company
Music setting by Richard Dawson Music Engraving
Printed in Hong Kong by Wing King Tong Co Ltd.

For permission to reproduce copyright material, acknowledgment
and thanks are due to TRO Essex Music Ltd. on behalf of John A. Lomax
and Alan Lomax for *All the pretty little horses*.

Every effort has been made to trace and contact copyright holders.
Should any omission have occurred, the publishers will be happy to
make the necessary correction in future printing.

THE KINGFISHER
NURSERY RHYME
SONGBOOK

With easy music to play for piano and guitar

COMPILED BY
SALLY EMERSON

MUSIC ARRANGED BY
MARY FRANK

ILLUSTRATED BY
MOIRA AND COLIN MACLEAN

Kingfisher Books

NEW YORK

CONTENTS

BABY GAMES

ACTION RHYMES

FAVORITE FIRST SONGS

DANCING GAMES

LULLABIES

DANCE THUMBKIN DANCE

Dance, Thumbkin, dance,
Dance, Thumbkin, dance.
Thumbkin cannot dance alone,
So dance you merry men every one.
Dance, Thumbkin, dance.

FINGER PUPPETS
Make little faces for your fingertips with sticking plaster, peanut shells, paper, or felt.

☆ *Waggle the thumb on its own, tucking the four fingers into the palm; then waggle all fingers; then the thumb on its own again. Repeat the game with each finger. Either help your child to perform the actions, or put on a show yourself.*

Other verses

Dance, Pointer, dance,
Dance, Pointer, dance.
Pointer cannot dance alone,
So dance you merry men every one.
Dance, Pointer, dance.

Dance, Longman, dance *etc.*

Dance, Ringman, dance *etc.*

Dance, Baby, dance *etc.*

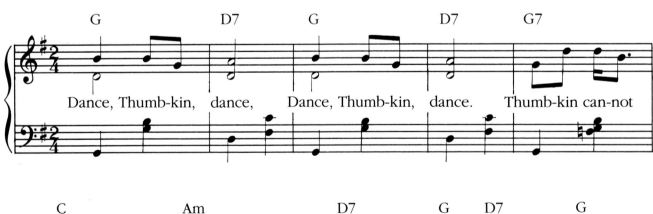

Dance, Thumb-kin, dance, Dance, Thumb-kin, dance. Thumb-kin can-not dance a-lone, So dance you mer-ry men ever-y one. Dance, Thumb-kin, dance.

THIS LITTLE PIG

This little pig went to market,
This little pig stayed at home,
This little pig had roast beef,
This little pig had none,
And this little pig cried:
Wee-wee-wee-wee-wee,
All the way home!

☆ *An old favorite – count
from big to little toe as
you sing and end with a
tickle.*

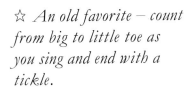

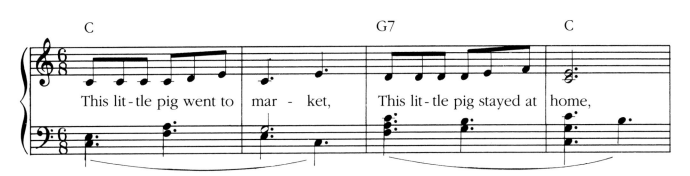

This lit-tle pig went to mar - ket, This lit-tle pig stayed at home,

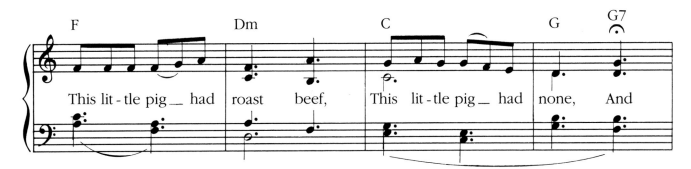

This lit-tle pig __ had roast beef, This lit-tle pig __ had none, And

this lit-tle pig __ cried: Wee - wee wee - wee - wee, All the way home!

PAT-A-CAKE

Pat-a-cake, pat-a-cake, baker's man,
Bake me a cake as fast as you can;
Pat it and prick it and mark it with B,
And put it in the oven for baby and me.

☆ *A hand-patting game for babies and a first
clapping song for toddlers. Act out the rhyme
by pretending to prick the baby's palm
and tracing a B on it.
Encouraging children to clap in time to the music is a good way
to develop rhythm and helps them realize that their hands as
well as their voices make excellent instruments.*

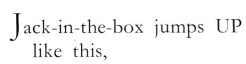

JACK-IN-THE-BOX

Jack-in-the-box jumps UP
 like this,
 ☆ *Swing baby up high.*

He makes me laugh when he
 waggles his head,
 ☆ *Shake him gently.*

I gently press him
 down again,
 ☆ *Lower him down.*

But Jack-in-the-box
 jumps UP instead.
 ☆ *Swing him up again.*

☆ *Up to eighteen months,
the best songs for babies are those
that involve swaying,
rocking, bouncing, and holding.*

Jack - in - the - box ____ jumps | UP like this, He

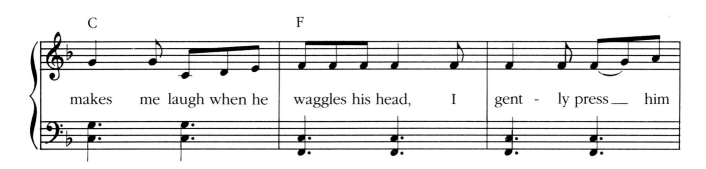

makes me laugh when he | waggles his head, I | gent - ly press ___ him

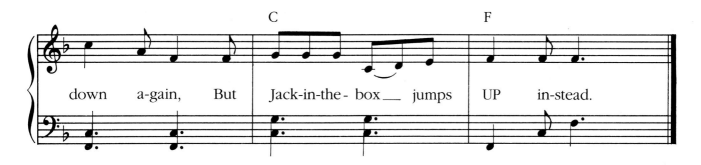

down a-gain, But | Jack-in-the- box ___ jumps | UP in-stead.

LAZY LUCY

What shall we do with a lazy Lucy?
What shall we do with a lazy Lucy?
What shall we do with a lazy Lucy?
Early in the morning?

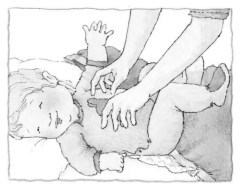

♫ *The same tune as*
"What shall we do with
a drunken sailor?"

Roll her on the bed and tickle her all over,
Roll her on the bed and tickle her all over,
Roll her on the bed and tickle her all over,
Early in the morning.

Heave ho and UP she rises,
Heave ho and UP she rises,
Heave ho and UP she rises,
Early in the morning.

MUSIC FOR BABIES

*Play any favorite music, from ballet to rap, while dancing with your small baby
in your arms. If the baby is restless or irritable, some romantic or energetic
dancing can calm and entertain you both.*

Roll her on the bed and tic-kle her all o - ver, Ear - ly in the morn - ing.

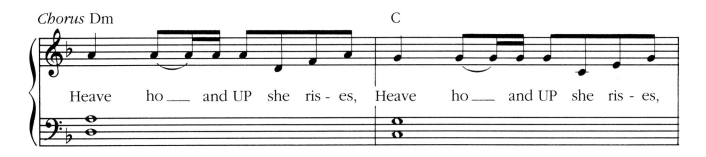

Chorus

Heave ho — and UP she ris - es, Heave ho — and UP she ris - es,

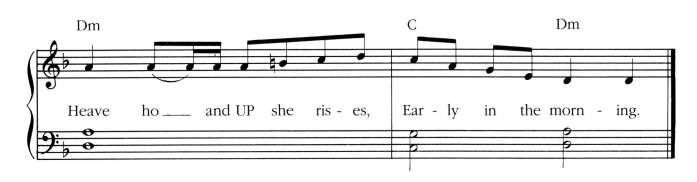

Heave ho — and UP she ris - es, Ear - ly in the morn - ing.

HICKORY DICKORY DOCK

Hickory, dickory dock,
The mouse ran up the clock.
The clock struck one,
The mouse ran down,
Hickory, dickory, dock.

☆ *Mime the mouse by running your fingers up and down the child's arm. Tickling songs are good for cheering up grumpy babies and toddlers.*

ROW YOUR BOAT

Row, row, row your boat,
Gently down the stream,
Merrily, merrily, merrily, merrily,
Life is but a dream.

☆ *Rock small babies from side to side. Pull older ones up to a sitting position and drop them gently down again.*

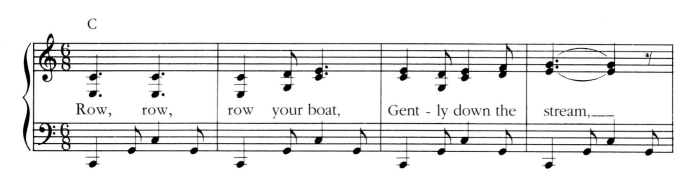

C

Row,   row,   row   your boat,   Gent - ly down the   stream,____

G   C

Mer-ri-ly, mer-ri-ly,   mer-ri-ly, mer-ri-ly,   Life is but a   dream.____

♫ *Two children can sit holding hands, with knees drawn up or legs crossed, pulling each other back and forth in time to the music. "Row, row, row your boat" makes a good round song too – see page 35.*

15

THIS IS THE WAY THE LADIES RIDE

This is the way the ladies ride,
Nimble nim, nimble nim, nimble nim;

This is the way the gentlemen ride,
Gallop a trot! Gallop a trot! Gallop a trot!

This is the way the farmers ride,
Jiggety jog, jiggety jog, jiggety jog;

This is the way the butcher boy rides,
Tripperty trot, tripperty trot, tripperty trot,

Till he falls in a ditch with a flipperty flop,
Flipperty flop, flop, FLOP!

☆ *Sit your child on your knees and bounce her up and down, mimicking the rhythm of the different rides. End by suddenly dropping the child between your knees. Babies can be bounced or rocked in your arms.*

☆ *As with all these songs, new verses can be added, substituting for example the child's own name to make the song more personal.*

TINGA LAYO

Tinga layo! Come,
little donkey, come.
Tinga layo! Come,
little donkey, come.

Me donkey BUCK,
Me donkey LEAP,
Me donkey KICK,
wid him two hind feet.

♫ *Repeat this verse.*

Tinga layo! Come,
little donkey, come.
Tinga layo! Come,
little donkey, come.

18

la - yo! Come, lit - tle don - key, come, Tin-ga

la - yo! Come, lit - tle don - key, come.

☆ *Trot your baby on your knees or hold him in your arms; lift him forward at* BUCK, *up at* LEAP, *and backward at* KICK.

HOBBY HORSE
You can make a simple hobby horse out of an old sock stuffed with newspaper on the end of a broom handle or length of dowel — sew on button eyes, felt ears, and yarn for a mane. Even using just a plain broom or stick, children will enjoy mimicking the different rides of "Tinga layo" and "This is the way the ladies ride."

19

EENTSY WEENTSY SPIDER

Eentsy Weentsy spider,
Climbing up the spout;
Down came the rain
And washed the spider out.

Out came the sunshine
And dried up all the rain;
Eentsy Weentsy spider,
Climbing up again.

☆ *With wiggling fingers mime the spider climbing*
UP and rain washing the spider DOWN.

☆ *Make a big circle for the sun and wiggle*
your fingers for the spider climbing UP again.

20

TWO LITTLE DICKY BIRDS

1 2 3 4

Two little dicky birds,   One named Peter,   Fly away, Peter!
Sitting on a wall,   One named Paul.   Fly away, Paul!

5 6

Come back, Peter!   Come back, Paul!

Two | lit - tle dick - y birds, | Sit - ting on a wall,

One named Pe - ter, | One named Paul. | Fly a-way, Pe - ter!

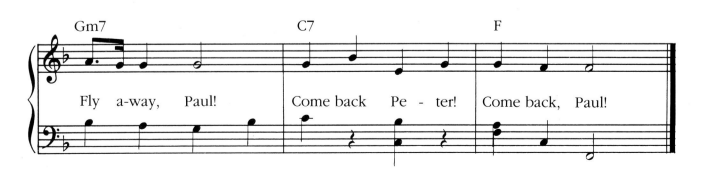

Fly a-way, Paul! | Come back Pe - ter! | Come back, Paul!

THE ELEPHANT GOES

The elephant goes
like this, like that,

He's terribly big,
And he's terribly fat.

1

2

3

He has no fingers,
He has no toes,

But goodness, gracious,
what a nose!

☆ *Toddlers will enjoy
acting out this rhyme
for themselves.*

4

5

6

The el - e -phant goes like this, like that, He's ter-rib - ly big, And he's ter-rib - ly fat. He has no fin - gers, He has no toes, But good - ness, gra - cious, what a nose!

I'M A LITTLE TEAPOT

I'm a little teapot,
Short and stout,
Here is my handle,
Here is my spout.
When I see the teacups,
Hear me shout:
Tip me over and pour me out!

☆ *Sing with actions.*

I'm a lit - tle tea - pot, Short and stout, Here is my han-dle, Here is my spout.

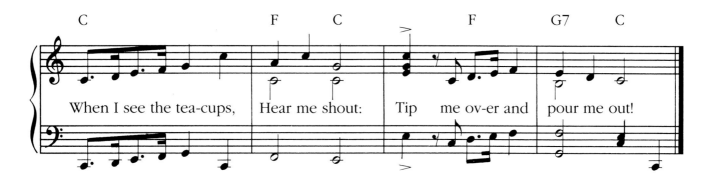

When I see the tea-cups, Hear me shout: Tip me ov-er and pour me out!

DUKE OF YORK

Oh, the grand old Duke of York,
He had ten thousand men.
He marched them up
to the top of the hill
And he marched them down again.

Chorus
And when they were up they were up,
And when they were down they were down,
And when they were only half-way up
They were neither up nor down.

Other verses
Oh, the grand old Duke of York,
He had ten thousand men.
They beat their drums
to the top of the hill
And they beat them down again.

They played their pipes
to the top of the hill *etc.*

They banged their guns
to the top of the hill *etc.*

♪ *Repeat the chorus
after each new verse.*

☆ *Sit your baby or toddler on your lap and
walk his legs or jog in time to the song.
Swing him* UP *and* DOWN *at those words.
Older children will enjoy marching in time,
jumping* UP *and crouching* DOWN, *and
acting out the additional verses or joining in
with their own musical instruments.*

DRUMS

Help a baby beat a saucepan or plastic bowl with a spoon. For older children, find a big empty can with a lid and decorate it. They can experiment with different beaters – a wooden spoon, paintbrush, chopsticks, egg whisk, and so on.

FIVE IN THE BED

There were five in the bed and
the little one said: Roll over! Roll over!
So they all rolled over and one fell out.

Other verses
There were four in the bed *etc.*
There were three in the bed *etc.*
There were two in the bed *etc.*

There was one in the bed and
that little one said:
♫ *Spoken, not sung:*
Good, now I've got the bed
to myself, I'm going to
stretch and stretch and stretch!

☆ *Both of these rhymes can be acted
out with five children, or toys; the toys
can be knocked in turn off a shelf, which will
strike young children as enormously comical.*

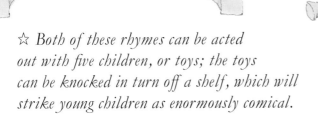

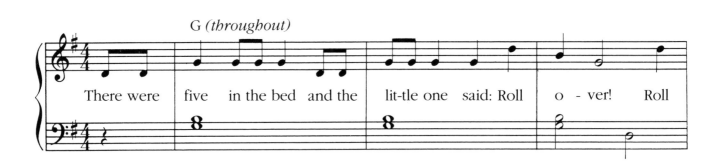

There were five in the bed and the lit-tle one said: Roll o - ver! Roll

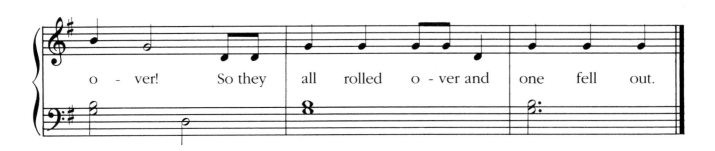

o - ver! So they all rolled o - ver and one fell out.

FIVE BROWN TEDDIES

Five brown teddies sitting on a wall,
Five brown teddies sitting on a wall,
And if one brown teddy should accidently fall,
There'd be four brown teddies sitting on a wall.

Other verses

Four brown teddies sitting on a wall *etc.*
Three brown teddies sitting on a wall *etc.*
Two brown teddies sitting on a wall *etc.*

One brown teddy sitting on a wall,
One brown teddy sitting on a wall,
And if one brown teddy should accidently fall,
There'd be no brown teddies sitting there at all!

♪ *The same tune as "Ten green bottles."*

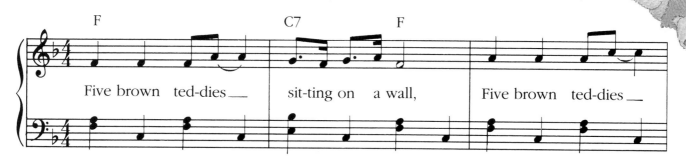

Five brown ted-dies ___ sit-ting on a wall, Five brown ted-dies ___

sit - ting on a wall, And if one brown tedd - y ___ should

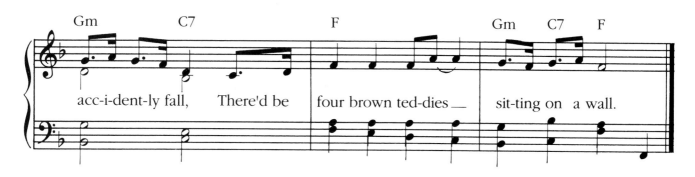

acc-i-dent-ly fall, There'd be four brown ted-dies ___ sit-ting on a wall.

WHEELS ON THE BUS

The wheels on the bus go around and around,
Around and around, around and around.
The wheels on the bus go around and around,
All day long.

☆ *Rotate arms like wheels.*

The wipers on the bus go swish, swish, swish,
Swish, swish, swish, swish, swish, swish.
The wipers on the bus go swish, swish, swish,
All day long.

☆ *Wave hands from side to side.*

The wheels on the bus go around and around,

Around and around around and around. The wheels on the bus go

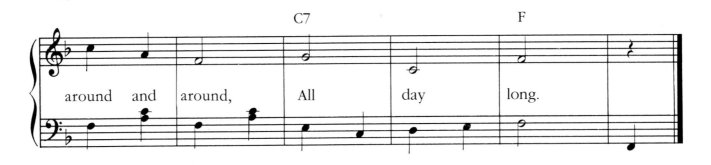

around and around, All day long.

TOOT TOOT

Other verses
The driver on the bus goes:
    Toot, toot, toot *etc.*
  ☆ *Press imaginary horn with thumb.*

The people on the bus go:
    Yakkity-yak! *etc.*
  ☆ *Open and shut fingers and thumb.*

The children on the bus make
    too much NOISE *etc.*
  ☆ *Hands over ears and shout* NOISE.

The babies on the bus fall
    fast asleep *etc.*
  ☆ *Head on hands as if asleep, and whisper lines.*

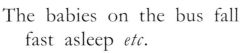

29

FRÈRE JACQUES

I HEAR THUNDER

Frère Jacques, Frère Jacques,
Dormez-vous? Dormez-vous?
Sonnez les matines,
Sonnez les matines,
Din, din, don! Din, din, don!

♫ *A very popular round song –*
see page 35. The English alternative
below can be sung to the same tune,
with actions.

I hear thunder, I hear thunder.
Hark, don't you? Hark, don't you?
Pitter patter raindrops,
Pitter patter raindrops,
I'm wet through, so are you.

I see blue skies, I see blue skies,
Way up high, way up high.
Hurry up now sunshine,
Hurry up now sunshine.
I'll soon dry, I'll soon dry.

FRÈRE JACQUES  I HEAR THUNDER

F *(throughout)*

Frè - re Jac-ques, Frè - re Jac-ques, Dor-mez vous? Dor-mez vous?
I hear thun-der, I hear thun-der, Hark, don't you? Hark, don't you?

Son-nez les mat-i - nes, Son-nez les mat-i - nes, Din, din, don! Din, din, don!
Pit-ter pat-ter rain-drops, Pit-ter pat-ter rain-drops, I'm wet through, so are you.

☆ *Actions for "I hear thunder:"*

1st verse
Drum with hands or feet; stop and
listen; flutter fingers; hug, as if cold . . .

2nd verse
Look up, and point to the sky; make the
circle of the sun; shake hands dry.

BIG BASS DRUM

Oh, we can play on the big bass drum,
And this is the way we do it:
BOOM, BOOM, BOOM goes the big bass drum,
And that's the way we do it.

☆ *Older children may like to add the*
noise of a new instrument with each
verse until they have the whole band.

Oh, we can play on the little flute,
And this is the way we do it:
TOOTLE TOOTLE TOOT goes the little flute,
And that's the way we do it.

Oh, __ | we can play on the | big bass drum, And this | is the way we | do it:

BOOM, BOOM, BOOM goes the | big bass drum, And | that's the way we | do it.

Other verses

TING TING TING
    goes the tambourine *etc.*

FIDDLE DIDDLE DEE
    goes the violin *etc.*

TICKA TICKA TECK
    go the castanets *etc.*

ZOOM ZOOM ZOOM
    goes the double bass *etc.*

TA TA TARA
    goes the bugle horn *etc.*

A HOME ORCHESTRA

"Big bass drum" does not literally need a violin or double bass. Any instruments, made or bought, will do. Simple ones to make at home include: dateboxes for clappers; wooden blocks for rhythm sticks; paper wrapped around a comb and blown with pursed lips; a series of bottles containing different amounts of water and struck with a spoon for chimes; a cardboard tube for a trumpet; small plastic pots and baby food jars, or large matchboxes, filled with dried beans, rice, beads, pebbles, or sand for shakers and rattles. (Make sure the containers are well sealed, as babies can choke on small beans and beads.)

Or use different parts of the body: stamp your feet, cluck your tongue, slap your thighs or knees, clap your hands . . .

BAA, BAA, BLACK SHEEP

Baa, baa, black sheep,
  Have you any wool?
Yes, sir, yes, sir,
  Three bags full;

One for the master,
  And one for the dame,
And one for the little boy
  Who lives down the lane.

THREE BLIND MICE

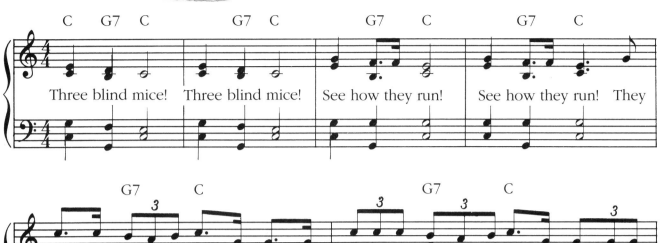

Three blind mice! Three blind mice! See how they run! See how they run! They

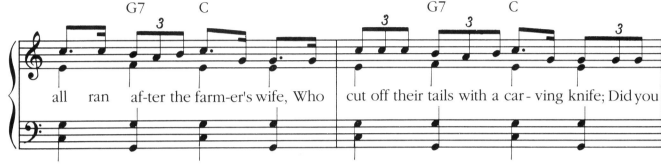

all ran af-ter the farm-er's wife, Who cut off their tails with a car-ving knife; Did you

ev - er see such a thing in your life, As three blind mice?

Three blind mice! Three blind mice!
See how they run! See how they run!
They all ran after the farmer's wife,
Who cut off their tails with a carving knife;
Did you ever see such a thing in your life,
    As three blind mice?

♫ *This can be sung as a round song: after the first singer has sung the first line, the second singer starts while the first continues on to the next line. Children love round songs, although they may quickly get muddled.*

HUMPTY DUMPTY

Humpty Dumpty
  sat on a wall,
Humpty Dumpty
  had a great fall;
All the King's horses
And all the King's men,
Couldn't put Humpty
  together again.

☆ *Use a toy on a shelf to represent Humpty and knock it off at* FALL. *Even babies and sweet-natured toddlers will delight in his catastrophe.*

Hump-ty Dump-ty sat on a wall, Hump-ty Dump-ty had a great fall;

All the king's horses, And all the king's men, Couldn't put Humpty to-geth-er a-gain.

POLLY PUT THE KETTLE ON

Polly put the kettle on,
Polly put the kettle on,
Polly put the kettle on,
We'll all have tea.

Sukey take it off again,
Sukey take it off again,
Sukey take it off again,
They've all gone away.

SING A SONG OF SIXPENCE

Sing a song of sixpence,
   A pocket full of rye;
   Four-and-twenty blackbirds,
     Baked in a pie.

When the pie was opened,
   The birds began to sing;
   Wasn't that a dainty dish,
     To set before the king?

The king was in his counting-house,
   Counting out his money;
The queen was in the parlor
   Eating bread and honey.

The maid was in the garden,
   Hanging out the clothes,
When down came a blackbird
   And pecked off her nose.

☆ *Happy ending:* Along came Jenney Wren
               And stuck her nose back on again.

LITTLE BOY BLUE

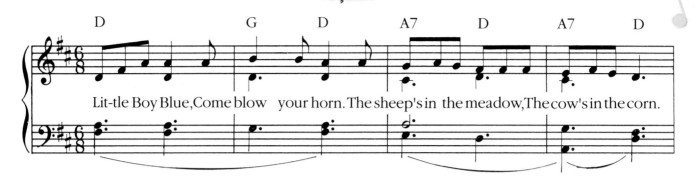

Lit-tle Boy Blue, Come blow your horn. The sheep's in the meadow, The cow's in the corn.

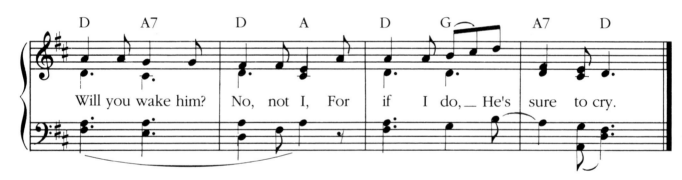

Where's the boy Who looks af-ter the sheep? He's un-der a hay-stack, Fast a-sleep.

Will you wake him? No, not I, For if I do, — He's sure to cry.

Little Boy Blue,
   Come blow your horn.
The sheep's in the meadow,
   The cow's in the corn.
Where's the boy
   Who looks after the sheep?
He's under a haystack
   Fast asleep.
Will you wake him?
   No, not I,
For if I do,
   He's sure to cry.

40

LAVENDER'S BLUE

Lavender's blue, dilly, dilly,
  Lavender's green;
When I am king, dilly, dilly,
  You shall be queen.

Lav - en - der's blue, dill-y, dill-y, Lav - en - der's green;

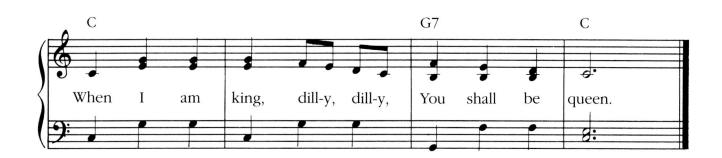

When I am king, dill-y, dill-y, You shall be queen.

Call up your men, dilly, dilly,
  Set them to work,
Some to the plow, dilly, dilly,
  Some to the cart.

Some to make hay, dilly, dilly,
  Some to thresh corn,
Whilst you and I, dilly, dilly,
  Keep ourselves warm.

POP GOES THE WEASEL

Up and down the City Road In and out the Ea - gle, That's the way the money goes, Pop goes the wea-sel! Half a pound of tup-penny rice, Half a pound of trea - cle, Mix it up and make it nice, Pop goes the weas - el!

☆ *Go* POP! *with finger inside your cheek — particularly good for amazing crying babies and making them forget what they were crying about.*

Up and down the City Road,
  In and out the Eagle,
That's the way the money goes,
  Pop goes the weasel!

Half a pound of tuppenny rice,
  Half a pound of treacle,
Mix it up and make it nice,
  Pop goes the weasel!

YANKEE DOODLE

☆ *Fun for knee rides and bouncers:*

Yankee Doodle came to town,
　Riding on a pony;
He stuck a feather in his cap
　And called it macaroni.

First he bought a porridge pot,
　And then he bought a ladle,
And then he trotted home again
　As fast as he was able.

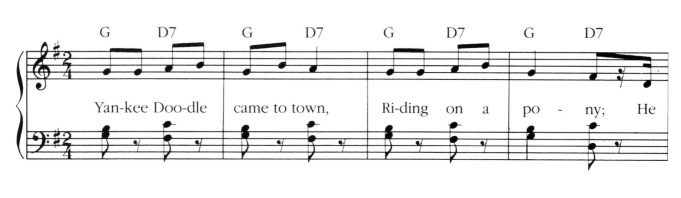

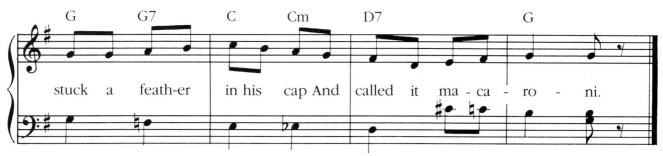

OLD MACDONALD

Old Macdonald had a farm,
E-I-E-I-O.
And on that farm he had some cows,
E-I-E-I-O.
With a moo-moo here,
And a moo-moo there,
Here a moo, there a moo,
Everywhere a moo-moo,
Old Macdonald had a farm,
E-I-E-I-O.

☆ *Repeat the song with different animals and noises.*

Old Macdonald had a farm,
E-I-E-I-O.
And on that farm he had some sheep,
E-I-E-I-O.
With a baa-baa here,
And a baa-baa there,
Here a baa, there a baa,
Everywhere a baa-baa,
Old Macdonald had a farm,
E-I-E-I-O.

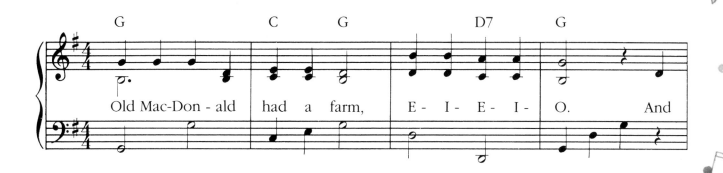

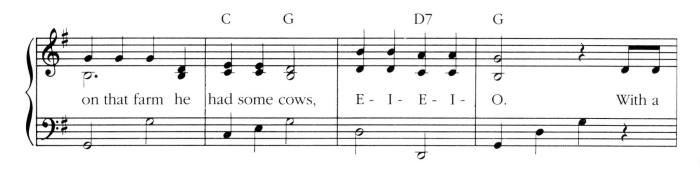

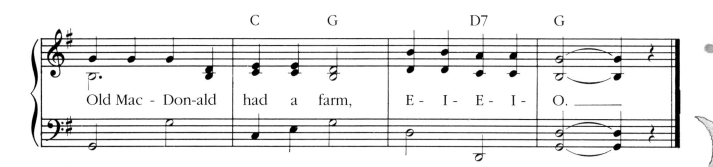

RING O' ROSES

Ring-a-ring o' roses,
A pocket full of posies,
A-tishoo! A-tishoo!
We all fall down.

☆ *Choose either of the next two verses*
to start again. Older children will love
the race in the second.

The cows are in the meadow,
Eating buttercups,
A-tishoo! A-tishoo!
We all get up.

The cows are in the meadow,
Eating all the grass,
A-tishoo! A-tishoo!
Who's up last?
NOT ME!

46

ONE LITTLE ELEPHANT

One little elephant went out one day,
Upon a spider's web to play;
He had such tremendous fun,
He sent for another elephant to come.

Two little elephants went out one day,
Upon a spider's web to play;
They had such tremendous fun,
They sent for another elephant to come . . .

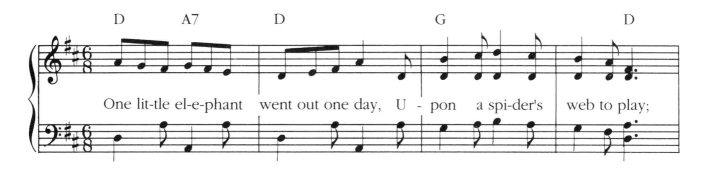

One lit-tle el-e-phant went out one day, U - pon a spi-der's web to play;

He_ had such_ tre - men-dous fun, He sent for a-noth-er el-e - phant to come.

☆ The French version:

Un éléphant se balançait,
Sur une toile d'araignée,
Il trouva ça si amusant,
Qu'il appèla un autre éléphant.

☆ An action game for lots of children. The first
ELEPHANT walks around swinging one arm like
a trunk. At the end of the first verse, the first
ELEPHANT chooses a second ELEPHANT who
holds on to him with her "trunk." Continue
until everyone is an ELEPHANT.

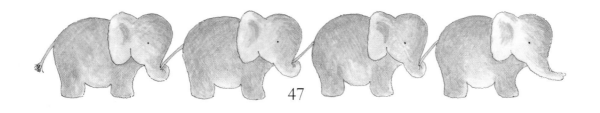

MULBERRY BUSH

MUSICAL STATUES

This popular game is an excellent way to encourage listening to music. When you stop playing the piano, or guitar, the dancers must stop exactly where they are, without moving a muscle, like statues. Send out any wobbly "statues" and start the music and dancing again. Be tactful with small children, who may not like being sent out.

You can of course play this game to recorded music.
Try all kinds – classical, folk, reggae,
jazz, pop, anything children enjoy dancing to.

Here we go round the mulberry bush,
The mulberry bush, the mulberry bush,
Here we go round the mulberry bush,
On a cold and frosty morning.

This is the way we wash our hands,
Wash our hands, wash our hands,
This is the way we wash our hands,
On a cold and frosty morning.

Other verses

This is the way we wash our face *etc.*

This is the way we brush our hair *etc.*

This is the way we clean our teeth *etc.*

This is the way we put on our clothes *etc.*

☆ *Join hands and dance in a circle. Stop to do the actions of the next verse. Repeat the first verse and its dance as the chorus after each new verse.*

49

HOKEY COKEY

You put your right arm in,
Your right arm out,
Your right arm in,
And you shake it all about,
You do the Hokey Cokey,
And you turn around,
That's what it's all about.

Chorus
Oh, the Hokey, Cokey, Cokey!
Oh, the Hokey, Cokey, Cokey!
Oh, the Hokey, Cokey, Cokey!
Knees bend,
Arms stretch,
Ra! Ra! Ra!

☆ *Everyone stands in a circle and follows the actions as they sing the verses. For the chorus, join hands and dance into the middle and out three times, bend knees, stretch out arms, and shout* RA! RA! RA!

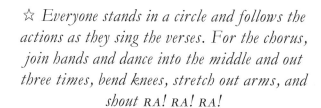

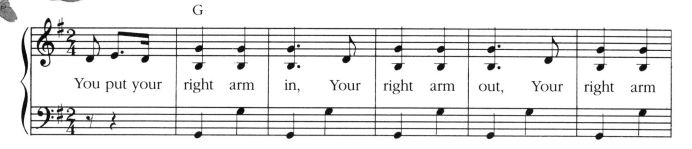

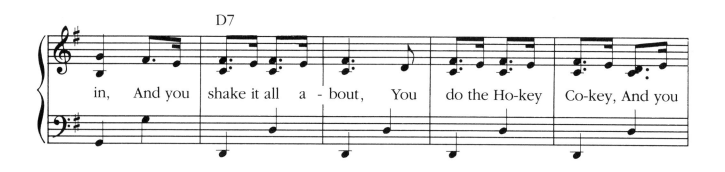

You put your left arm in *etc*.
You put your right leg in *etc*.
You put your left leg in *etc*.
You put your whole self in *etc*.

ra ra ra

ANKLE BELLS
Sew some little bells onto two bands of elastic tape or ribbon and slip them on over the ankles, to make dancing even more fun.

You could use wooden beads or macaroni on one ankle, to make a different noise from the bells on the other.

Chorus G

Oh, the Ho-key, Co-key, Co-key! ___ Oh, the

Ho-key, Co-key, Co-key! ___ Oh, the Ho-key, Co-key,

Co-key! ___ Knees bend, Arms stretch, Ra! Ra! Ra!

THE FARMER'S IN THE DEN

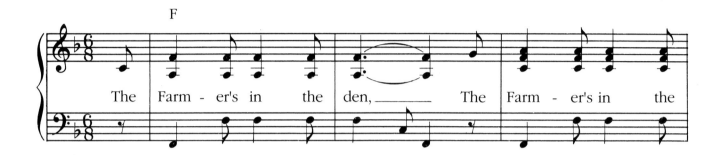

The Farmer's in the den,
The Farmer's in the den,
Eee-Aye-Eee-Aye,
The Farmer's in the den.

The Farmer wants a Wife,
The Farmer wants a Wife,
Eee-Aye-Eee-Aye,
The Farmer wants a Wife.

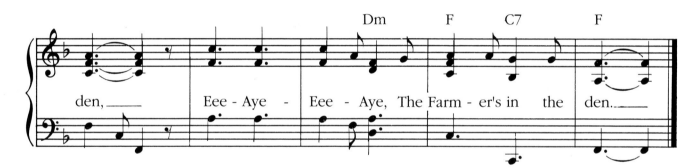

Other verses
The Wife wants a Child *etc.*
The Child wants a Nurse *etc.*
The Nurse wants a Dog *etc.*
The Dog wants a Bone *etc.*
We all pat the Bone *etc.*

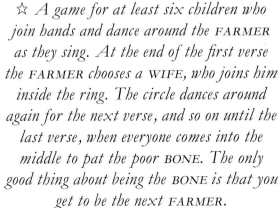

☆ *A game for at least six children who join hands and dance around the* FARMER *as they sing. At the end of the first verse the* FARMER *chooses a* WIFE, *who joins him inside the ring. The circle dances around again for the next verse, and so on until the last verse, when everyone comes into the middle to pat the poor* BONE. *The only good thing about being the* BONE *is that you get to be the next* FARMER.

OATS AND BEANS

Oats and beans and barley grow,
Oats and beans and barley grow.
Do you or I or anyone know,
How oats and beans and barley grow?

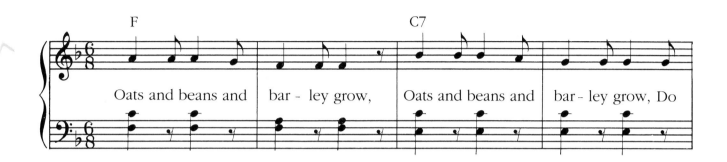

Oats and beans and | bar - ley grow, | Oats and beans and | bar - ley grow, Do

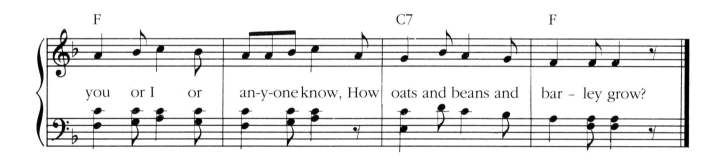

you or I or | an-y-one know, How | oats and beans and | bar - ley grow?

First the farmer sows his seed,
Then he stands and takes his ease,
Stamps his feet and claps his hands
And turns around to view the land.

☆ *The* FARMER *stands in the middle of the ring. Everyone dances around for the first verse. Then the* FARMER *pretends to* SOW *the seed,* STANDS *with his hands on his hips,* STAMPS *his feet and* CLAPS *his hands, and* TURNS AROUND *to look at his land.*

ORANGES AND LEMONS

Oranges and lemons,
Say the bells of St. Clements.
  I owe you five farthings,
    Say the bells of St. Martins.
When will you pay me?
Say the bells at Old Bailey.
    When I grow rich,
      Say the bells at Shoreditch.
When will that be?
Say the bells of Stepney.
    I'm sure I don't know,
      Says the great bell of Bow.

☆ *Two children form an arch (or two adults, if the children are too small). One side of the arch will be Oranges, the other Lemons. The rest skip around, under the arch. At the last line, the arch pretends to* CHIP *and* CHOP *the children as they pass through and captures one at* HEAD. *The captive chooses Oranges or Lemons, and stands behind whichever side he has chosen. The game is repeated until everyone has been captured. Then the two teams, Oranges and Lemons, have a tug of war.*

Here-comes-a-candle-to-light-you-to-bed,
Here-comes-a-chopper-to-chop-off-your-head,
♫ *Spoken, not sung:*
Chip-chop-chip-chop-the-last-man's HEAD.

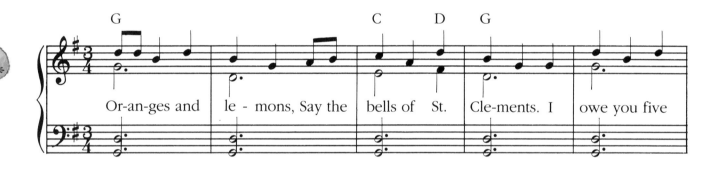

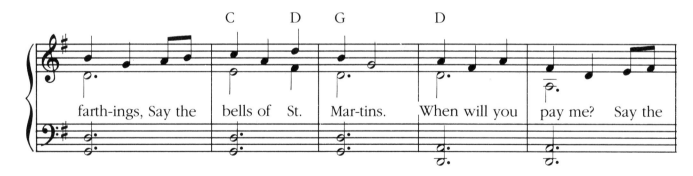

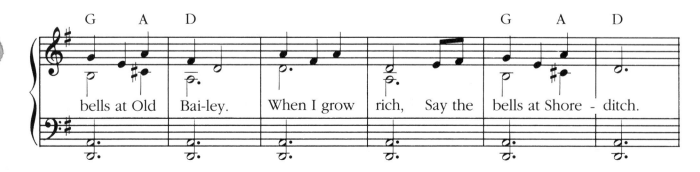

54

HUSH-A-BYE

Hush-a-bye baby on the tree top.
When the wind blows, the cradle will rock;
When the bough breaks, the cradle will fall;
And down will come baby, cradle and all.

☆ *Rock your baby gently in your arms as you sing this old cradle song.*

Hush - a - bye ba - by, on the tree top.

When the wind blows, the cra - dle will rock;

When the bough breaks, the cra - dle will fall; And

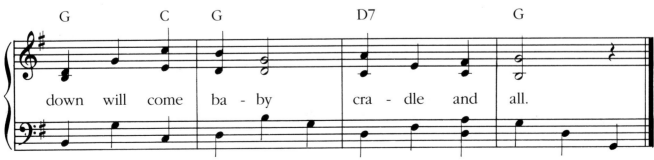

down will come ba - by cra - dle and all.

DANCE TO YOUR DADDY

☆ *Sung boisterously, this lullaby also makes a good knee ride or bouncer
for babies who are not yet sleepy.*

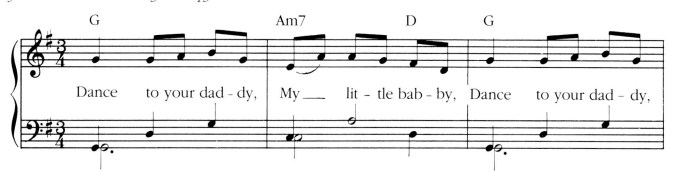

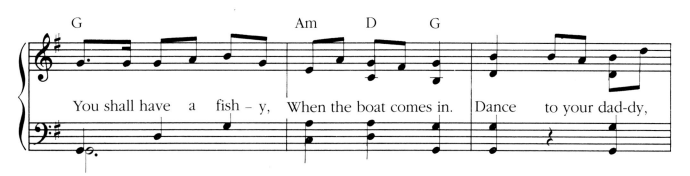

Dance to your daddy,
My little babby,
Dance to your daddy,
My little lamb.

You shall have a fishy,
In a little dishy,
You shall have a fishy,
When the boat comes in.

SLEEP, BABY, SLEEP

Sleep, baby, sleep.
Thy father guards the sheep;
Thy mother shakes the dreamland tree,
Down falls a little dream for thee;
Sleep, baby, sleep.
Sleep, baby, sleep.

Sleep, baby, sleep.
The large stars are the sheep;
The little stars are lambs, I guess,
The gentle moon's the shepherdess;
Sleep, baby, sleep.
Sleep, baby, sleep.

Sleep, ba-by, sleep, Thy fa - ther guards the sheep; Thy

moth-er shakes the dream-land tree, Down falls a lit - tle dream for thee;

Sleep, ba - by, sleep. Sleep, ba - by, sleep.

ALL THE PRETTY LITTLE HORSES

Hush-a-bye,
   don't you cry,
Go to sleepy,
   little baby.

   When you wake,
      you shall have
   All the pretty
      little horses.

Blacks and bays,
   dapples and grays,
Coach and six of
   little horses.

Dm · Gm · C7 · F · Gm · Dm

Hush-a - bye, · don't you cry, · Go to slee-py, lit-tle · ba - by.

Dm · Gm · C7 · F · Gm · Dm

When you wake, · you shall have · All the pre-tty lit-tle · hor - ses.

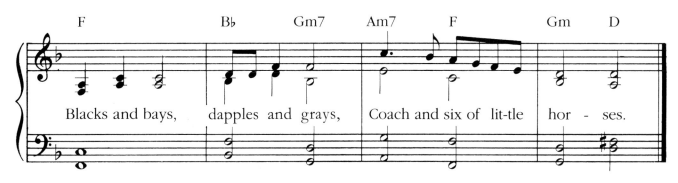

F · B♭ · Gm7 · Am7 · F · Gm · D

Blacks and bays, · dapples and grays, · Coach and six of lit-tle · hor - ses.

MOCKINGBIRD

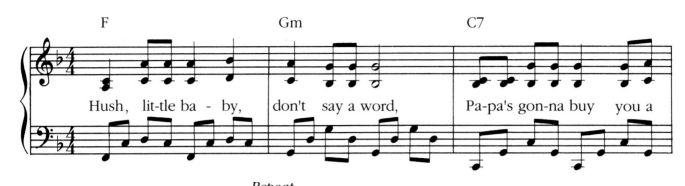

Hush, lit-tle ba - by, don't say a word, Pa-pa's gon-na buy you a

Repeat

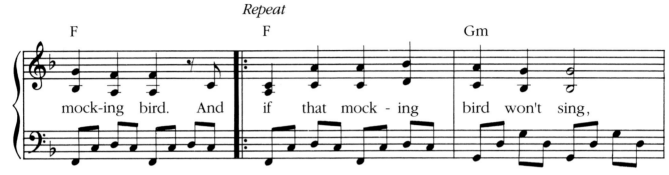

mock-ing bird. And if that mock - ing bird won't sing,

Pa - pa's gon - na buy you a dia - mond ring.

Hush, little baby, don't say a word,
Papa's gonna buy you a mockingbird.

And if that mockingbird won't sing,
Papa's gonna buy you a diamond ring.

If that diamond turns to brass,
Papa's gonna buy you a looking glass.

If that looking glass gets broke,
Papa's gonna buy you a billy goat.

If that billy goat won't pull,
Papa's gonna buy you a cart and a bull.

If that cart and bull turn over,
Papa's gonna buy you a dog named Rover.

If that dog named Rover won't bark,
Papa's gonna buy you a horse and cart.

If that horse and cart fall down,
You'll still be the sweetest baby in town.

GOLDEN SLUMBERS

Golden slumbers kiss your eyes,
Smiles awake you when you rise.
Sleep, pretty wantons, do not cry,
And I will sing a lullaby:
Rock them, rock them, lullaby.

Care is heavy, therefore sleep you;
You are care and care must keep you.
Sleep, pretty wantons, do not cry,
And I will sing a lullaby:
Rock them, rock them, lullaby.

THOMAS DECKER

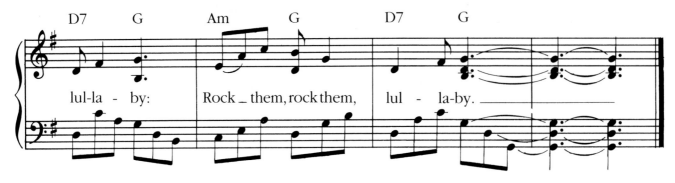

KUM BA YAH

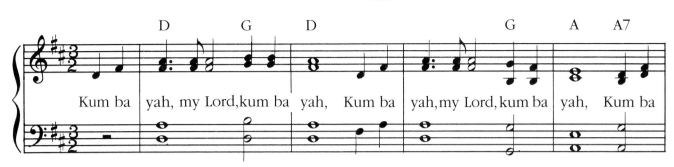

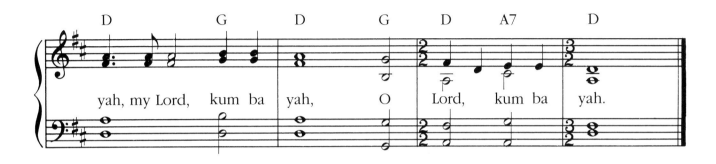

Kum ba yah, my Lord, kum ba yah,
Kum ba yah, my Lord, kum ba yah,
Kum ba yah, my Lord, kum ba yah,
   Oh Lord, kum ba yah.

Someone's singing, Lord, kum ba yah,
Someone's singing, Lord, kum ba yah,
Someone's singing, Lord, kum ba yah,
   Oh Lord, kum ba yah.

SCARBOROUGH FAIR

Are you going to Scarborough Fair?
Sing parsley, sage, rosemary, and thyme.
Remember me to one who lives there,
For once she was a true love of mine.

Are you go - ing to Scar - bor-ough Fair? Sing pars - ley,

sage, rose - mar - y, and thyme. Re - mem - ber me to

one who lives there, For once she was a true love of mine.

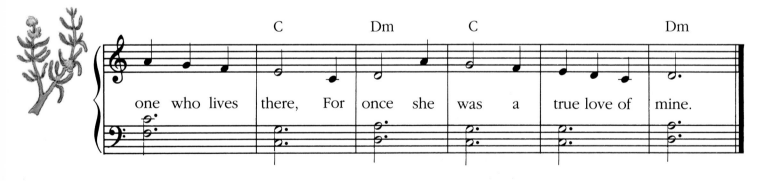

Tell her to buy me an acre of land,
Sing parsley, sage, rosemary, and thyme.
Beneath the wild ocean and
   yonder sea strand,
And she shall be a true love of mine.

Tell her to make me a cambric shirt,
Sing parsley, sage, rosemary, and thyme.
Without any stitching or needlework,
And she shall be a true love of mine.

Tell her to wash it in yonder dry well,
Sing parsley, sage, rosemary, and thyme.
Where water ne'er sprung nor a
    drop of rain fell,
And she shall be a true love of mine.

Tell her to dry it on yonder sharp thorn,
Sing parsley, sage, rosemary, and thyme.
Which never bore blossom since
    Adam was born,
And she shall be a true love of mine.

MUSICAL STORIES

Lullabies are love songs for babies — any soothing song you know and love can be sung as a lullaby. It is flattering how much a child likes even the most unmusical parent's voice.

Before older children go to bed, you might sometimes listen to music together and make up stories to go with it. In this way, instead of reading a bedtime book, a child can hear the princess escaping or the sun rising.

Try describing the music (is it fast or slow, loud or soft, jumpy or sleepy?) and ask the child how the piece makes him or her feel.

BABY'S BOAT

1 Ba-by's boat's a sil - ver moon Sail - ing in __ the sky, by.
2 Sail-ing o'er a sea of sleep While the stars float

Chorus

Sail, ba - by, sail Out u-pon that sea;

On - ly don't for - get to sail Back a-gain to me.

Ba - by's fish - ing for a dream, Fish - ing far and near. ____ Her

line a sil - ver moon-beam is, Her bait a sil - ver star.

Repeat Chorus

Baby's boat's a silver moon
Sailing in the sky,
Sailing o'er a sea of sleep
While the stars float by.

Chorus
Sail, baby, sail
Out upon that sea;
Only don't forget to sail
Back again to me.

Baby's fishing for a dream,
Fishing far and near,
Her line a silver moonbeam is,
Her bait a silver star.

Chorus
Sail, baby, sail
Out upon that sea;
Only don't forget to sail
Back again to me.

BRAHMS' LULLABY

JOHANNES BRAHMS

Lullaby and goodnight,
In the sky, stars are bright.
Around your head, flowers gay
Scent your slumbers till day.
May you wake when the day
Chases darkness away,
May you wake when the day
Chases darkness away.

Lullaby and goodnight,
Let angels of light
Spread wings around your bed
And guard you from dread.
Slumber gently and deep
In the dreamland of sleep,
Slumber gently and deep
In the dreamland of sleep.

INDEX OF FIRST LINES